SLEEPING DOGS

By the same author:

Peripheral Vision
Clouds and Edges

SLEEPING DOGS

MARTIN DOLAN

RECENT
WORK
PRESS

Sleeping Dogs
Recent Work Press
Canberra, Australia

Copyright © Martin Dolan 2020

ISBN: 9780648834366 (paperback)

 A catalogue record for this book is available from the National Library of Australia

All rights reserved. This book is copyright. Except for private study, research, criticism or reviews as permitted under the Copyright Act, no part of this book may be reproduced, stored in a retrieval system, or transmitted in any form by any means without prior written permission. Enquiries should be addressed to the publisher.

Cover image: © Martin Dolan 2020
Cover design: Recent Work Press
Set by Recent Work Press

recentworkpress.com

SS

Contents

1. Voices from Uruk

Aruru contemplates her work	3
Shamhat remembers Enkídu	4
Enkídu among the animals	5
Gilgamesh contemplates his dual nature	6
Gilgamesh listens for the gods	7
Humbaba among the cedars	8
Shamash renounces his devotee	9
Uta-napishti contemplates eternal life	10
Uta-napishti's wife	11
Gilgamesh loses the flower of immortality	12

2. Sleeping Dogs

Rimbaud in Marseille, 1891	15
Memento mori	18
Maes Howe	20
Sleeping dogs	21
Always giving offence	22
Declension	23
Winter through telescopic sights	29
What the lance-corporal said	30

3. Decaying Orbits

Black powder	33
Metamorphoses	35
Easter	37
Event horizon	41
Jellyfish	43
December sky	44
Faraday cage	45
Decaying orbits	46

The astrophysicist to his love	47
Three laws of thermodynamics	48
Locked room	49
Meat puppets	50
Uncanny valley	51
On drinking to forget	52
Schrödinger's cat	53

4. Rights of reply

Farewell: Mr Thomas Responds To Dylan	57
Prospero, Later	59
Good Fences Make Good Neighbours	60
Jean Armour's Song	62
Now I Am Old And White	63
Penelope	64
Dear Andrew	66
At The Summer Solstice	68
After The Frost	70

Afterword	73

1. VOICES FROM URUK

Aruru contemplates her work

They weave and scurry like cockroaches
towards their next mating, their next meal,
forgetting why it was we made them,
the hard work of digging and tilling.

They are nothing but clay mixed with blood:
dug-up clay and blood from one of us.
I can see his angry, fearless eyes
as we cut his throat and drained him dry.

We made them to serve us. They do not.
They talk and laugh, showing no respect
as we sit alone in our temples,
waiting for worship that never comes.

I can accept all but the laughter.
My gift to them to soften their toil
they have now thrown back in my face,
mocking the careful order of things.

I will press new clay with cut fingers
until it is softened with my blood,
shape a new man to stride among them,
and breach their defences like a flood.

Shamhat remembers Enkídu

First of all you must know that he stank:
not of sour wine, sex and nervousness
like the clients I knew in brothels.
No, he stank of drying mud and dung,
of old piss and half-digested grass.

I smelt him coming before I saw
him slip from the herd and sidle up
to where I sat and then hesitate,
step back. There was work I had to do
and the promised pay outweighed the stink.

It was easy. I laid out some bread,
white, soft, on a plate with oil and salt
and a cup of wine poured from a flask.
Then I stripped, slowly—that was my job
—and laid myself down on my dropped clothes.

There was nothing subtle about him.
He ate my food. He drank, then we fucked
in all his strange stink of the farmyard
while his eyes darted back to the herd
then returned to me, fascinated.

Afterwards I talked and he listened
as though words and thoughts were new to him
and he did not know how to use them.
The herd all ran from him, afterwards.
The stink lingers. He will not forgive.

Enkídu among the animals

Before you came I was as silent as clay
moving here, stopping there with the grazing herd.
When hunger came I ate then later I shat.
I walked to the waterhole, drank, tasted mud.
I could run forever and none could catch me.
I saw the traps you dug and I filled them in
was unclothed and did not know I was naked
was happy and needed no words to say it.
Now I am weak and slow like a little death
and the herd scatters and runs for fear of me.
I too should run, for I know what pursues me
now you have given me the words to name it.

Gilgamesh contemplates his dual nature

I do not remember my mother.
Endless faces come to my mind's eye,
sometimes bidden, sometimes not, slipping
into the tablets of each night's dream
or walking the length of walls with me
as sun beats down. So many ghosts
jostling with the living. Never her.
So many ghosts and my dead father
most of all. He made the human part.
My vanished mother made me a god
and I am more god than not, they say,
but they—living, dead, by day or in dream—
cannot tell me what is man, what god,
which part of me takes son from father
and smashes him to a senseless pulp,
takes daughter from mother and rapes her.
Why will no-one come here to stop me?
The king is dead and so I am king.
Ninsun is gone that made me a god
made me feared and so made me alone.
I do not remember my mother.
Why will no-one come here to stop me?

Gilgamesh listens for the gods

Each day I visit the house of a god
or a goddess. I listen in the dark
to the snuffling priests, the shuffling footsteps
of servants, muttered prayers, money clinking.
I smell the dung of animals waiting
for the knife, smell the blood from their cut throats,
the smoke and the char of the burnt offerings.
I listen in the dark for some answer
to heaped-up sacrifice, to chanted prayer.
No answer comes.
                        Only the evening comes
as a scout for the armies of the night,
then night itself and sleep and the riddles
the gods set for us in the guise of dreams:
stars fall, turn into unliftable rocks;
an axe is throned beside me like a king;
whole mountains crush me and ash covers me.
Those silent gods send dreams to mock me, send
nightmares that make my heart thrash in my chest,
gather like flies round our sacrifices.
They roil and they buzz but they say nothing,
they do nothing.
                  I lose count of the days,
lose grasp on my patience. I know my dreams.
There are forests to cut, bulls to slaughter,
a city to be ruled. I know the price.

Humbaba among the cedars

When they sent me here I looked into the pool
that spreads the colour of sky towards those cliffs
and the face of a stranger looked back at me
with a monster's fierceness and an exile's pain.
These days I close my eyes when I bend to drink
and do not open them until I look up
to the mountains where wind serries the cedars
and higher up where the snow shrinks from summer.
I can stand for hours just breathing in the scent
of transpiring leaves, breathing out the anger
of the thousand slights of being neither god
nor man, but both. I can live among these trees,
touching their needles, resin sharp on my tongue.
Such trees should never be wood. I will guard them
and watch the unmade paths for signs of strangers.

Shamash renounces his devotee

I did not ask anything of anyone,
walking the length of daylight from dawn to dusk
in careful lines: the comfort of the foreseen
that is the only gift I can ever give.
Still he pushes up prayers, pours libations
as though I could give more than the certainty
of a daily course, the messiness of dreams
he makes into stories, takes as messages.
Sometimes the winds will blow and he will thank me.
He will kill a bull and offer me its heart,
singed in holy fires—but it is he who eats,
not me. It is he who acts since I cannot,
though he does not know it, will not recognise
our lack of power. Tonight Enkídu will die
when my daylight loses power. He will go down
into the darkness he fears, the forgetting
that hides in the house of dust where they eat clay.
There is nothing to be done but incise this
on clay, carve it on walls. Perhaps they will last.

Uta-napishti contemplates eternal life

I had grown used to stone men with stone faces,
how they pushed paddles hard at water, soldiers
training relentlessly for the next battle,
one whose outcome is both fated and unknown.
I have lived long enough to have forgotten
who they once were, where they came from to take up
rowing on the chill glassy waters of death.

So now he comes, one who shattered stone bodies
and left my boatman helpless, he comes in rage
and grief and fear. He cannot tell them apart.
He poles the boat with question after question
that he brings to me as though they were demands.
He wants to live forever; he wants to know
what I could have done to merit such a gift.

I will tell him my story. He will believe,
fully, because everything I say is true,
but it is not everything and so not true.
He will fail, humanly, needing sleep and dreams.
He will fail again because he is a god,
needing to be beautiful. He will never ask
if I wanted the gift, either then or now.

The gods said their gift was to live forever.
All they gave was not dying. I am still here
with my wife, with my store of goods, not dying,
answering all their questions with a story
that never has an ending. Perhaps someone
will bring me an answer in exchange.
Let it be well-aimed, with a sharp edge.

Uta-napishti's wife

I did not ask for any of this. To live
so far away, to live for so long.
No one knows my name, remembers how
I was funny and clever, how I was loved.
He told me to leave, so I left
with him. The gods let us live, made us
live and live. They put a sea of death
between us and those we loved. They left.
We wait here until the cold-eyed men
—always men—come with their empty hands
seeking the gift that we cannot give.
I cook, bake bread. I wash. I listen
to the same stories that never end.
I offer advice and they take it
with their cold eyes and hangdog looks
and they leave. I want to go with them
but I stay and hear the old story
and hope for a different ending.

Gilgamesh loses the flower of immortality

It truly was an ugly thing, that flower,
uglier than the monsters that crowd the edge
of too many nights without sleep, too many
days of staring uselessly into distance.

I had lost my friend and was afraid to die
so I reached out for the ugliness of life
that bloomed like a flower under drowning waters,
hidden among relics of the oldest flood.

That flower had thorns far worse than a briar,
my hands were slashed and welted from grasping it.
I took it with me, blood dripping from my hand,
saying with each step *Enkidu is still dead*

and I am living still and afraid to die.
Each step that was one more towards that city
where they wait for me patiently, expectant
that I will order things to meet their desires.

In the end I slept, then woke when the sun rose.
The flower of life was beside me, ugly
and sharp as before. I left it lying there
and went to wash my dirty face, my cut hand.

When I came back it was gone. I cried loudly
but in truth I did not care. Some things are worth
the seeking after and the pain. This was not.
The city waits for me to go or to stay.

2. SLEEPING DOGS

Rimbaud in Marseille, 1891

1. *Limbs of iron*

> *Je reviendrai, avec des membres de fer*

Each day they take something more from me
and I always lose on the exchange.
Yesterday they took my leg and left
agony as interest on pain
already stored up. The day before,
they stripped the south away, rag by rag,
leaving only the grey sky and rain
that I thought I had outrun. And yet
there are some things that they will not take,
that I cannot lose. Mother is there
in the corner, dressed in black, mouthing words
from the book I tried to throw away.
No, she is gone. She leaves when I wake
screaming in a mess of sweaty sheets.
She wants my money. She has never
wanted me, only her idea
of who I could be. I have nothing
for her, except this body of iron
and the words that are starting to creep
from nightmare onto a bloodstained page.

2. Frightful vigil

Pitoyable frère ! Que d'atroces veillées je lui dus !

Lamplight skates across my wrist, traces out veins,
shadows the lines of tendon. Sometimes it aches,
as though half-knitted bones were grinding themselves
into shape. A perfect circle of grey skin
marks where your bullet hit, where my blood pulsed out.
Now fingers can curl and straighten. I can make
a fist, give the finger to the night, give it
to you, as though you were here, with your bottle
of oil, your pathetic fish. I can still see,
when I wish to, how you stood outside the door,
all forlorn and domestic. Of course I laughed.
Of course you hit me with your dead fish. The scales
scratched my face. I remember that fish better,
feel it more than any memory of you,
of your straggling hair, your failure of a beard,
clay pipe, cheap tobacco. Your vacillation.
I remember money, never quite enough,
doled out by your mother. I have money now,
but they won't tell me where it is. You hit me
with your fish and ran all the way to Brussels.
I sold your clothes, grabbed your books and followed you,
having no money, nothing better to do
than share that madness with you. And then the gun,
waved wildly towards your temple, waved wildly
at me, two shots, my wrist shattered and a hole
in the wall to show you could not shoot me twice.
I wrote what I wrote. So did you. But I stopped,
truer than you to madness. Nothing is left
except the ache of my wrist bones. Somewhere near,
tobacco burns. I hated your stupid pipe.

3. Saddest dreams

Je dus voyager, distraire les enchantements

Where is my ivory? I bought tusks,
long brown teeth torn from dead grey giants.
I paid for them with twenty-five days
of desert, with a sap-smelling crate
of long guns slippery with grease.
Sharpness of oil, sourness of old sweat
splutter and chink of harnessed horses.
Where is my ivory? Clicking balls
on green baize, plink and chording of keys,
the jingle of the gold I earned
and used to buy teeth. O ivory
of the old gates through which false dreams come,
false dreams and bright nightmares of fever,
pain in the leg which is gone, taken
like the slaves that I bought with guns
and sold for gold, tusks of ivory.
None of this counts for the scribbling clerks
in Paris, slowly losing empire.
I scribbled, once upon a far time.
I stopped. The clerks scratch on forever.

Memento mori

One morning, another was in the mirror
looking back at you, but he was no stranger:
grandfather, uncle, someone you knew as old;
had this been painted, there would have been a skull.

*

When you constructed worlds with lenses and light
you took care to keep us out, friends and others,
but we were always there in the trampled grass,
in stones that were once built up, in stones torn down.

*

Because you lived long enough, we told your life
as though your last ten years had never happened
as though you had left for some backward country
from which little news came, slow and always late.

*

We have laid you down in a spread of bodies
and called it memory. We have raised a mound
of dirt softer than flesh in the falling rain;
the binding grass grows that others will come to cut.

Skara Brae

Rain whimsies down the wind
lacquers the hides of cows
that graze by standing stones
and rasp up wads of grass.

The cows crunch and slobber
while sheep, white like maggots
crawl across the green hills
under inconstant clouds.

Sun sneaks into full light
over cool folds of bay.
The buried village wears
draggle of centuries.

Bickering over games
on the beach, children build
not sandcastles but huts
corbelled from round grey stones

modelling the village.
Sand will bury or waves
will undermine their work
until huts are piled stone

scattered by winter waves.
Sun stays an afternoon;
cows stamp and steam, sheep writhe;
a bus grinds up the hill.

Maes Howe

Arnfithr the son of Stein carved these runes
he and his mates eight hundred years ago
when they dug into the chambered tomb
closed up four thousand years before them.

The saga says it was dead of winter.
The setting sun reaches out then, enters,
splashes the farthest wall with reddish light.
Two of the many were mad by night's end.

No sign of that in the runes. *Thorni fucked.*
Helgi carved. Sharp scratchings from a long night's
stopover in transit south. *Thorir was here.*
The Mediterranean was waiting.

Long ago a treasure was hidden here.
Simon Sirith carved that, but stone and water
are all that is left for those coming after
—and fingers of sun on a winter wall.

Sleeping dogs

A stone dog at the feet of its stone
master, all signs of slobber and bounce,
of hair and foul breath and wagging tail
smoothed away by the mason.

Such cool, marmoreal sleep. Utter
stillness among the years of shuffling
crowds, of muttered responses to stubs
of worn-out ceremony.

Pagan kings took slaughtered dogs with them,
still warm, into graves or burning ships;
pharaohs took cats on their last journey
as though to some clear purpose

but this carved effigy lies asleep,
no sign of watchfulness, no ear pricked,
stiff as its master on a cold tomb
emptied now even of bones.

Always giving offence

We lived there, at home in our damp rooms:
the cooking smells, the coal fires, closeness.
Someone took offence, maybe at how
we talked or how we stood together
outside. Or how we laughed. Someone built
this place to collect us, divide us.
We made our new marks, together
in new places. Always giving offence.

Declension

1. Nominative

The first name you gave her was always secret
as the little clump of cells grew large, as bones
hardened under the softness of growing limbs,
the curve of torso. You kept it to yourself.

The second name was hers. She has taken it,
now that she makes words sound through pharynx, take shape
from tongue and lips, reach out to possess the world.
She has taken her name. It is hers, not yours.

She takes her name. She takes the words you give her.
She is voracious in her pursuit of more,
of ways to call things by their truest names.
He, though, the father, keeps his words to himself.

He watches her silently then turns and goes
out into the light and wind, to the animals
that are his world. She does not yet know their names
but she will learn them all before he is gone

2. *Vocative*

O, you say. O. Your mouth shapes the sound
that should bring his gaze back towards you.
Dogs will lollop up when you call them,
while birds fuss and squabble at the feeder

but he gives no sign that he has heard
where he leans on the decrepit gate.
It is cold and the wind blows the smoke
of others' warmth through the muddy yard.

Clouds shiver over the sun, pass by.
You call his name. He turns with the slow
care that is still his. He walks to you,
his cheeks wet from the wind in his eyes.

3. *Accusative*

You say all this is just what occurs
to you, to him. You widen your eyes
as though helpless. He offers silence
enough to meet downcast certitude.

The child who formed, grew in your body,
plays happily in her world that has
no philosophy yet. She builds blocks
into walls, towers. She brings them down.

The next thing will occur, and the next.
The moon will rise, as though the huge earth
did not move. The child will sleep and you
will lie, waiting for the world to turn.

4. *Genitive*

You have lived here long enough. Long enough
to have breathed and shitted, pissed, sweated
away the last atoms of elsewhere
until even your bones are local.

It is not enough. You cannot say
so easily that this is your place
although, absent, you pine for clear light
and grow sick for the wind in these trees.

You cannot say that this is your place
even though day by day it buys you
with the small change of air and water
a debt that must be repaid in kind.

Not even the child who was formed, grew
in this place, the child you call yours
though you are hers, not even she gives
you claim to this place that she will leave.

5. *Dative*

Every year he hands you a gift
folded around the forgotten time
when you began. On another day,
between winter and spring, he will bring

memory in an envelope, words
written by someone else, printed
and regular, and it is enough
for the day, to mark another year

meshed together, inextricable.
His gifts are beautiful, sometimes.
Yours are practical, as he wishes.
You keep them, sometimes give them away

and he uses his until they break
or he tires of them. Every day
you watch to see what the day will bring:
something is given or something gives.

6. *Ablative*

The days pass. Each scrapes some skin from you
and hides it as fluff in the corners.
You pass the days in endless movement
without ever leaving here
though every atom is stripped and replaced.

Always leaving, whether from the spot
you and he constructed as your fixed point
or from vague provisional places,
you seemed to walk side by side
though lines from the same point must diverge.

You will always go away, leaving
a thin trail of tiny things behind
to lie like pebbles or scattered crumbs.
Dark birds hug the branch, waiting.
No need yet for another good-bye.

Winter through telescopic sights

These mornings of clutching cold,
frost sparkling as it catches
thin sunlight, you can see steam
rise above the latrines there:
men in field grey piss, unseen.
This steel loophole has distilled
pure cold from the night and gnaws
gloved fingers as they scrabble
numbly towards their purpose.
They are so distant, those hands,
disconnected, driven by
the spring of their own clockwork.
One takes the sack-wrapped barrel
of the rifle, the other
works the bolt, smoothly, then drops
to wait, loose on the trigger.
The cross-hairs shift, curious,
seeking oddness in the white.
Shadows move, clockwork fingers
squeeze, a head explodes, red spray.
That was not your eye searching
not you in those hands. The job
is over, done, done again.

What the lance-corporal said

Of course we were drinking. That's what pubs are for
after a winter's day learning how to kill
so that we wouldn't have in think about it
when the time came. A grey day. Dreich. There was snow
up in the mountains and the cold searched us out.
So cold the sergeant-major stopped his shouting
and whispered to us how to slide the knife in,
how to swing the cosh and just where it should hit.
The cosh was my weapon. Smash in their temple
or the back of their skull. I didn't like knives
the way John did. You get too close to a man
when you use a blade, so close you can feel them,
breath hot on your cheek. Yes, John preferred the knife.
And so we were all drinking, always drinking
the whisky warming our guts, heating our thoughts
and John got too close to one of us. I won't
say who it was. He punched John and John walked out
into the cold. We staggered back to barracks.
We didn't miss him until morning parade.
We went searching. I found him first, by the loch.
Face down. Dead. Cold as the wind or the water.
The back of his skull caved in as though he had
fallen back, drunk. Yes, someone could have hit him,
killed him. We all knew how. Who'd do such a thing?

3. DECAYING ORBITS

Black powder

1. *Sulphur*

Soft crystals grow, yellow as butter,
grow and flower near vents and craters
where steam and stink of brimstone
mark the spot where lava lurks, brooding.

Like quicksilver, these once were magic,
held the hope grey lead could turn to gold
but now are gathered and crushed
into puffed mounds of lung-scratching dust.

2. *Charcoal*

Entire forests were felled to get this,
were felled and stripped, piled up and covered
so fire could work in secret,
airless, its sacrament of carbon.

So light, so lifeless these grey-black blocks
pulled from hiding by smudged, coughing men
and broken up for fuel
for drawing or turning into dust.

3.	*Saltpetre*

A year turns piss into mineral
if done right: stale in buckets of hay;
wait for a slow bloom on straw;
wash through ash and dry in glinting piles.

The fastidious prefer bat caves
where the crystals scraped from ancient shit
can be heaped and broken up:
from waste to bright prisms then to dust.

4.	*Gunpowder*

In their endless search for endless life
the alchemists compounded powder
of brimstone, char and nitre
and brought their houses down around them.

Tubed tight behind round iron or lead
the means at last defeated the end.
Each new firework celebrates
the elixir of mortality.

Metamorphoses

1. Madder

Begin perhaps with this: leaves sharp
and long as spear blades, fanned on stems
that hook and climb towards the light;
long roots that search and burrow down.
Dig them, dry them, crush and soak them
until they bleed red in the pot.

2. Woad

Or here: flopped green leaves, yellow flowers
crushed and steeped, fermented slowly
until the air stinks like spoiled eggs
until blue falls out through water
darker than sky or sea, lighter
than night—the blue stain of evening.

3. Linen

A young woman in a red shift
of linen dyed with rose madder
carries a baby in her arms.
She's so young for this, so trusting.
She wears a cloak of indigo:
evening is cool in this hill town.

4. Cinnabar

Go on perhaps to this: crystals
that will poison a careless hand,
that stink of sulphur when heated
and yield bright drops of mercury.
When crushed to powder, mixed with yolk
they shine out as vermilion.

5. Lapis

Or see men hack stones from mountains
and ship them west: stones bluer than sea
from the darkness where no sea is.
Craftsmen could carve stories from them
but instead countless hammerfalls
turn stone to ultramarine dust.

6. Birchwood

Finish here with a wooden board
planed smooth and gessoed thirsty white
where faith will work with alchemy
to change some teenager and child
to mother of god: heaven's blue
draped on the red of blood and birth.

Easter

1. Thursday

The routine of our family meal
requires only that we wash our hands
arrange a few plates and knives
sit down and share the everyday

so this later other meal
this supper of ritual and symbol
stuffed with centuries of meaning
inherited like old furniture

this meal misses its unsubtle point
about events in an upper room
shared lamb and wine, bread and herbs
bitter with contention and betrayal.

Here our feet are washed by others
washed with a punctilious tension
that outwardly and visibly belies
inward and invisible submission.

I washed my own feet this morning
like each morning that has gone before
whispering perhaps a hurried prayer
for the unwanted gift of servitude.

2. *Friday*

The liquid sunlight vacillates
between affirmation and cloudy denial.
Trees wait immobile and mute
for judgement and sentence.

The roads curve into emptiness.
Passers-by are distant and scattered
accidental to the landscape
walking as though happy.

Clouds gather in swirling mobs
demanding some significant event
matching their stormy response
to an inadequate afternoon.

As detached as a condemned thief
I join a murmured congregation
that is too polite to demand Barabbas
or even raise slim eyebrows

at the intrusion of foreign accents
around their communal brazier.
We wait together for more sunlight
to fill the world like a cock's crow

for some impossible quake or eclipse
to tear the shabby day apart
raise buried thoughts from their tombs
and send them talking through the world.

It will not happen. It does not.
The dead as always bury their dead
while the living shuffle off lifelessly
through a suddenly cloudless afternoon.

3. *Saturday*

Huddled together in shadow
as impersonal as the tomb
that tomorrow will be empty
we hear old stories again:

how light was divided from darkness
and worlds teemed and multiplied
how attempts at child sacrifice
are the true answer to a test

an answer whose future reward
is the drowning of whole armies.
We hear how water quenches thirst
how water will cleanse defilement.

We relive baptismal contradictions
washed clean in the waters of death.
Once more I hold my breath as if
drowning in the clarity of autumn.

4. *Sunday*

Rain rolls across another autumn
grey notes laying the slow blues
on dust that settles into mud.

Leaves cling stubbornly to green
until harder cold and longer dark
release the alchemy of fall.

An insinuating wind
carries conspiracies of winter
into the heart of our gathering.

This antithesis of spring
subverts Easter ritual
closes the sky like a tomb

so the greetings we exchange
wrapped in shiny politeness
are brittle as chocolate eggs.

Like the Magdalene we came
hoping to adorn cold facts.
We too are disappointed.

Event horizon

Remembrance has a gravity
that pulls all moments towards it
till we only know for certain
what light will remember for us.

The light will remember for us
how it was, before today's green
shrivelled, was clutched in drying sap
and wrapped in a twist of amber.

The light will remember for us
fixed on paper or in numbers
so we can let each moment go
in its long fall away from now.

Everything must pass

> *There is a needle 'I' between the past and the now through which everything must pass.*

Inga Clendinnen *Agamemnon's Kiss*

Years of dust have shuffled down in motes
so fine they will not be brushed away.
This is where you sat, and no one since.

It is time that you sat there again.
Let us talk as though you were here
and had sat to ease your weariness.

I am tired, too, and older
than you were when you died.
Sit across from me so we can talk

of those things that sons will never say
to fathers while they live, or of how
fathers find that strength is not enough.

Smell the scent of the rose bush
remember the cutting that I struck
from the bush my mother had planted.

But a scent cannot draw you back,
only the needle through which a thin past
could be threaded, if only my hand were steady.

Jellyfish

Past the break there is swell,
dip of ocean, dry taste
of salt, the weight of sun
as you swim through the day.

It floats like a soft bell
letting the blue light through.
Tentacles stretch and dangle
their whispers of venom

then clutch, wrap up the splash
of arms and legs. Panic
and pain make the day real.
Heartbeat. Thrashing to shore.

Vinegar takes away
stings, dulls day back to calm
sunlight, soft thump of waves,
gooseflesh from a cold breeze

but body remembers
for a long time, twitching
at each unexpected
touch, the tightness of sheets.

December sky

Lying on our backs at midnight, grass pricking
coolly through the thinness of our summer shirts,
marijuana competing for carelessness with beer
in our bloodstreams, pulses warming into mirth,
we watched the Geminids sear and scar the sky,
electric, unpredictable and silent.
There are still nights when I can lie on my back,
alone, staring up at the rotating stars,
willing them to stop wheeling, to slip and slide.
I remember how it felt, looking upwards,
vertiginous, like falling towards Saturn.

Faraday cage

When we are outside we feel the lightning build
in ugly clouds that jostle sparks from the ice,
filling air with tension and raising the hairs
on our bowed necks. Trees shiver uneasily
while the ground holds firm, waiting for the sharp bolts
to lash down stepwise from the thunderheads
and return, brighter, to the place they came from.
All in an instant, this will be, like a knife
from the dark. Such things can kill, but we have built
cages from our stores of mesh, held together
with flimsy twists of wire. Each has space for one
and each one takes their space alone, protected
from the crackling threat of the storm. We are safe:
no jagged lightning can get inside—or out.

Decaying orbits

Nothing can hold to a straight line through space;
Objects curve their paths towards each other
As though in travelling they would rather
Aim to congregate in one crowded place:
Some passing through, a simple change of pace
Before swinging out towards another;
Some circling as though around a lover;
Some spiralling towards a last embrace.
So too there are ways to approach a thought
That avoids expression: a single pass
That sprouts its meaning like a comet's tail
And fades; a fixed orbit when we are caught
By an idea; or the final crass
Impact of truth driven home like a nail.

The astrophysicist to his love

Under a curve of black sky, frost settles
on grass, crystal by crystal, glinting back
at the spread and swirl of inconstant stars

Reach out and take my cold hand in yours

All those stars should fall inward like apples
down wells of gravity until they are
indistinguishable, crushed into each other

Hold me, because I am lonely and cold

All stars should fall but do not. With slowness
that a year cannot measure they drift apart
pushed by unseen stuff that fills empty space

Kiss my eyelids; I do not want to see

The thing that fills empty space is darkness,
unseen and pushing everything away
until darkness alone is left, brooding

Oh love me till this dark, these stars are gone.

Three laws of thermodynamics

1.

We lie together this winter night
and eke out our warmth by holding close.
One day we can stop this give and take.

2.

When your warmth has matched itself to mine
we look to find another balance
as two thoughts draw themselves into one.

3.

Even the deepest sleep has its dreams
floating like grey fog over the frost
but we wake with none to remember.

Locked room

The walls in here are lined with cork.
The light is stark. The walls are white.
Nothing I try here seems to work
to make your absence good or right.

The voices in my head are loud
yet muffled so I cannot hear
a single word they say. They crowd
and crush. The stink they leave is fear.

I plug my ears against all sound
and hope the clock ticks round to day,
to silence. I hope you will be found.
The room is empty. Voices stay.

Meat puppets

Dry bones gathered, articulated
clothed in muscle and skin; dank sputum
or worse from a careless demiurge;
cool lumps of clay, shaped smooth and breathed on;

the universe playing dice, alone
endlessly. Sometimes they care, these sacks
of flesh, as they reach from first clumping
of cells to their last liquefaction,

sometimes they care, these frail meat puppets
as they bump, grind against each other
and make the air shiver with questions
with words that hang in empty spaces

that no embrace can bridge; these soft things
that twitch on the end of unseen wires
sometimes care enough to ask why not
and find new steps to dance, words to sing.

Uncanny valley

We give them dolls to play with, plastic
or porcelain, painted smiles, moulded
limbs, artificial hair and hard eyes
that stare, blink. Nothing behind the glass.
We teach them to draw faces, outlined
in crayon or pencil, brightly filled.
They scribble, making the familiar
distant, to be handled with care.
We give them photographs, cameras
to catch the world, catch themselves almost
perfectly, as they should wish to be.
In the gaps between not real enough
and too real is where dreams are, and fear.

On drinking to forget

Memory can be the opposite
of alcohol: distilled, concentrated
it gives the very thing that drinking
takes away. The two come together
in a bright flash of entropy.

Schrödinger's cat

Steel walls contain my every cry,
keep me immured, keep you outside:
do not look in, for I may die.

I've caterwauled, heaved out a sigh:
however long and hard I've tried,
steel walls contain my every cry.

Over there is the last goodbye:
a corked-up flask of cyanide.
Do not look in, for I may die.

That mirror must not catch my eye:
to see myself is suicide
though walls contain my every cry.

The Geiger counter cannot lie
about how chance might soon decide.
Do not look in, for I may die.

I watch myself; I'm my own spy:
alive or dead, I must decide.
Steel walls contain my every cry,
do not look in, for I may die.

4. RIGHTS OF REPLY

Farewell: Mr Thomas Responds To Dylan

If I'd foreseen this fuss before I died
His moaning as they took my corpse away,
I'd not have taught him as I did of pride

Since he does not understand. He may
Before another Rubicon is crossed
By his own death learn quietly to grow

To gentle age. Not everything is lost
Across that border or before, although
He's cried for loss since weaned from mother's breast.

Still, what happens to bodies underground,
However planted there, blessed or unblessed,
Is not the happiness he hopes I've found.

A slick coffin is nothing like a bed
And rot sets in some little time before
The worms begin their thing. And being dead

Is mostly boring. I see less than I saw
Half-blind on my deathbed by the sea.
(Half-sighted, too, to see that he was blind

With drink, as ever.) How is it that he
Could get such travesties into his mind
Of what it's like to fade in pain?

The morphine meant that when at last I died
I didn't notice. The moment wasn't plain
And delirium leaves no time for pride.

He cared much more than I for what I owned
And whether or not I had ever cried.
He is the one whose twisty words have wound

A bright legend from my unconscious glide
Into silence. His sort looks at the sky
And creates a place they hope we'll go.

Even sightless I cast a colder eye
Than he whose rhetoric floats like snow,
Who hears bright music from the silent spheres.

He wept at the passing of my last breath
And did not see how I gifted him tears
And images and words and rage at death.

Such rage because he knows he too will die
However he blusters and tries to hide
Himself in drink. He says I didn't cry.

Nor will I. There is space, here by my side.

Prospero, Later

I thought that you had set me free,
Sent me away so I could be
My simple self with all my faults:
Too weak to fight abuse, assaults;
Forgetfulness my only prayer
Against seductions of despair;
And no charm left that could enchant
Others to my wishes, my want.
Now my breath roughens, my sight fails;
I scan the horizon for sails
That might bring news into my hands
From the once-new world, from its bands
Of spirits freed from every spell,
But no sail comes, no news. I dwell
Amongst remnants of what I got
For coming back. But it is not
Enough. What I received from you
was no freedom that I could own:
By freedom I was overthrown.

Good Fences Make Good Neighbours

It was for him that I maintained this wall
and since he left I find no time for it.
I would watch pine trees brighten as the sun
caught them unawares; watch birds fly abreast
in twos and threes; watch any changing thing
before I'd turn mind or hand to repair,
to the rough heft of fallen lumps of stone.
Some things there are that should be brought from hiding
and opened to the light: the cruel, the mean,
the dark things twisted up in what we've made.
It seemed that he wanted to keep them there
enmeshed with those cold spirits of the hill
that whistled through his mind. He saw a line
of wall assaulted again and again
by nameless foes, against whom we would go
(in his crusader's mind), restoring each
rock to tidiness. Like juggler's balls—
moving just to maintain their place—we'd balance
stone on teetering stone until we'd turned
disorder back. He'd concentrate on them
—all the time pretending it was a game
to which there was no purpose any more—
as though a whole world turned on mending wall.
Sometimes I thought it was about his orchard
and stopping the world from reaching across
to steal apples. And somehow elves to him
were halfway real: subterranean neighbours
producing chaos in a flash of wonder.
There was a wall he had built in his head
past which I could not reach: the stretch of it
impervious and smooth. He talked of cows
we did not have, of things I did not know—
or so he said—that we were walling out
or in. When questioned he would take offence

as though at ignorance. Our drystone wall
held a world of significance for him
I was too benighted to see, or rather
was too intent with him on building there
the wall that now is crumbling from its top.
Those rocks with which he claimed to see me armed
had no hard constructive purpose for me:
I would as soon have thrown them to the trees;
and when I told him of my father's saying
about fences he missed that point as well:
fences do not need making good, but neighbours.

Jean Armour's Song

I've watched the fading of the rose
  You cut for her last June;
And how she played your melody
  Till strings fell out of tune.

She never was your bonnie lass,
  Nor any more am I:
Your deepest wish now seems, my dear,
  To drink that bottle dry:

Then drink another dry, my dear,
  And sprawl out in the sun,
Or stagger through the rain, my dear,
  My Tam who cannot run.

I'll stay here then, my only love,
  And watch our bairns a while,
May you come safe through rain, my love,
  And over each cold mile.

Now I Am Old And White

What moron told you that with age comes sleep?
In white-haired, wakeful age I take your book,
And quickly read, and picture the dumb look
That all you poets seemed to think was deep;

Recall your words in all their empty grace
And their unease with men whose deaths were true.
This reading once more stokes my rage with you
And all the mystic vagueness in your face.

You never saw the world through prison bars;
Faced with a republic's price, you fled,
Without pursuit or harpies overhead,
From death towards your gyring, worthless stars.

Penelope

An aged wife—queen to the raddled king
of subjects that he fears to rule, of crags
he grows too old to walk—I will not dole
my greying favours out to him, nor race
to draw another crowd of men to me
that he might kill again. I'll let him drink
and boast of all the women he enjoyed
while I protected hearth and crown from those
who sought them over twenty years. But when
this winter passes and the Hyades
have brought spring rain, I will recall my name
and cover up my face and veil my heart
and walk incognito among the men
and women that he scorns. The governments
he says he knew have taught him not at all;
the kings and princes that he claims as peers
because of squabbling years in front of Troy
would fail to recognise him if they met
him now and here. I know they'd see straight through
his restlessness; they'd see it's youth that fades,
not fame, and fading keeps him on the move.
Oh, yes! I'll walk abroad, and in the end—
for these are people knowing what's of use
and what's a waste—I'll find another life.
Submissive queen was not the role for me,
however long I played it. What is saved
from lives so long apart is nothing more
than skill at weaving: lies or cloth. We were
a mismatch from the start. I found myself
caught first by inexplicable desire
for his hair, red as the glowering star
that serves as eye for Taurus. Then I thought,
when lust was gone, that our Telemachus
could tie me to him still and to his isle.

But off he ran: promises to fulfil
or break; black lies to tell with face as mild
as summer seas; betrayal by degrees.
For twenty years I spoke no word but good
of what he did, how in the highest sphere
of politics and war he could not fail.
I knew at once there'd be some price to pay
for misplaced loyalty. I knew the gods
were playing at a game that was not mine
and I must lose, but I watched for his sail
and listened for hubbubs of mariners
and cheers for home. He says he thought of me
each day, each night—and every time he took
a lover, or so I choose to suppose,
for he came back to me though I am old—
almost as old as he—and bent by toil
before a weaving frame. There was an end
to wanderlust; philandering was done
and peace restored with all the fickle gods;
no more would sirens lure him on to rocks
or witches summon him across the deep.
But now he stumbles out to find new friends
(his old ones being drowned) to sail the world.
Such words he uses! "Purpose", "seek" and "smite"!
If these new friends could see what friendship holds
in store: the crushing, wounding, and the baths
in comrades' blood; a thousand ways to die.
And die they will. He always lets them down
and goes his own way. He will seek the isles
that he calls "happy" since he never knew
how to be happy here. He'll go, as though
his being king were nothing and his days
designed for fun. He'll go where phantoms are
and not come back to heal unbroken hearts.
I'll weave his shroud and live just as I will
and watch the waves to see what they might yield.

Dear Andrew

If you had ever made the time
to listen, then what seemed a crime—
my laboured thought, my measured way
of pacing through each hour of day—
should not have forced you from my side.
I would have said that moon and tide
should set the pace of love; I could
have met your sweet strength at its flood
when that time came. How could love refuse?
But you moved on. You thought the Jews
behind it all. I watched it grow,
your paranoia that my slow
and thoughtful speech, my cautious praise
came from plotting beyond your gaze;
that hidden here, between each breast
in fabric, you might find the rest
of some conspiracy. My part
was innocent: I heard my heart
and against it no plotting state
or learned protocol could rate.

We all hear what we want to hear
and what you thought you heard was near
insane—that or some other's lie
merits fire for eternity.
Whatever truth you thought you found,
my reason's clear, my case is sound.
If truth is what you want to try
please don't start with virginity:
you were not first, though he is dust
who first matched patience with his lust:
and others also have their place
ahead of you for my embrace.

No roses, then, of any hue—
hothouse limp or touched by the dew—
you know whatever now transpires
they'll be consigned to love's slow fires.
Some final advice if I may:
if you see me as some small prey
to give long chase to and devour
remember I keep all my power
of yes and no: not much, but all
I need. Face it. You've dropped the ball.
It's not me that's trouble and strife;
suck it up. Get on with life.
I deserve my time in the sun
but not with you. Goodbye. Must run.

At The Summer Solstice

What you have left me is words, and words only
without the charm of telling
that could so entrance a listening child;
you have left words that no longer belong
to any story's shining
out, that find no myth to nestle into.

I have scrutinised each one for such virtues
as it may retain from you
and have found nothing. Yours was an odd will,
bequeathing only sentences and turns
of phrase: I wanted your crown
of story-telling, to reign as you reigned

the king of bright tales as old as the ark,
as old as that first woman
who accepted the price, unfalteringly,
of choosing her own story and her own fate.
I wanted to give witness
to all the different ways that we can fall

like Lucifer, burning down in beauty,
Samson in Delilah's thighs
dreaming an earthquake into mass murder
or how you leapt, too, no longer smiling,
from darkness behind your back
through a window to the hard ground of love.

This was the madness from which I was hatched
as sun dipped into ocean
and started a journey of fifty springs
random as birds swerving through jostling reeds,
as uncertain as the night's
slow fading into day on an eastern shore.

Dawn of the longest day breaks, hollowly.
I am two years your elder
now, thirty years after you drank the cup
of forgetting. Summer spreads blue upward
as the sunlight confesses:
that you have left me cold words, and words only.

This should be a day for drink, for smiling,
for sudden gifts of flowers;
but half a world away, half a lifetime,
the longest night is dark and spray whips from wave.
There where the black sky is wild
your words might make stories, might be performed.

After The Frost

When you stopped your half-hearted ministry
to our family's joy, I did not cry;
I thought that things could be as before:
a perfect family at its perfect rest.
We knew a genius must find what suits
his inspiration, putting to one side
such luxuries as sitting peacefully
beside his sleeping children. What disturbs
a household's calm, you said, was calm. How strange.
And strange things drove you into the dark wood
that chokes the middle passages of life:
your calm, rapt contemplation of a flame;
the drugs that brought you dreams when sleep would not.
I'm old enough to know how love can grate
through simpleness, because everything
should be complex, be deep in very nature.
And so you found you could or would not live
with happiness in its domestic form;
children and wife were prison to a spirit
that sought the freedom of everywhere;
you found you valued freedom for itself
and left without a thought.

         At school, so often
I tried to bring your absent face to mind
and always saw a face concealed by bars,
though unsure who was outside, who in. Often,
Lonely for simple cottage warmth, I dreamed
I sat beside you in some high tower
or stayed with you in a pleasure dome that rang
with sunlight, with the excitements of a day
together. In dreams you would come to me
but not in life; at home my waiting ear
would never hear your hoped-for footsteps come.

It was as though the ice-caves that you dreamed
had crushed the hopes that budded in my dreams
or blighted them with frost before the morning.
Since what I wished for never filled my eye
I searched it out in each pamphlet or book
written by you. Each poem that I snatched
and read in my chilly room could lift me up
to a cold height where you could show your face,
where I could know myself held and beloved
where you could see how much we were alike.

I slept once in a cradle by your side
—or so you wrote—as you sat vexed by calm.
You hoped that I could fill the vacancies
that cracked the crazy paving of your thought.
Now you are twice removed from me: through heart
submitting to full exile from you;
through broken promise that I'd learn your lore.
Where now the baby you hoped to see reared
among ancient mountains? Why instead this dim
small world of the unwanted, of faint stars?
No scent of honeydew comes on the breeze;
no demon lovers stalk the icy crags;
no albatross keeps faith among the clouds.
I waited so long on your lonely shores,
waited for stories that I could not hear
or, hearing, could not make intelligible.
You offered me to the will of your God
who has never been mine, who could not teach
or show the smallest aspect of himself.
That God is in your image, from your mould;
like you he'll never give me what I ask.

Now you are dead as well as gone, now you
are underneath a hundred clods of earth
I hope you've found the world you used to sing:
where ice hung its shards from every branch

and hoar frost spread silver on the rustic thatch.
I'll watch your caves of ice until they fall
and crush your pleasure dome with that last blast.
I'm done with calm, I'm done with midnight frost
and this next spring will melt all icicles.
It's daytime now, though I still see the moon.

Afterword

Most of the poems in this collection give voice (or rather voices) to people who have not been given or have not been able to take up their rights of reply. Others—mostly poets—have said things about or to these people that available evidence indicates were misplaced or distorted.

The work that opens with the words *Sha naqba īmuru* (He who saw the abyss), and that we misguidedly call the Epic of Gilgamesh, like most ancient texts attributes little in the way of an internal life to its characters. The poems of the first section take as their starting point the assumption that complex characters have rich internal lives.

It is puzzling to look at the cleavage between the teenage Rimbaud, whose imagination and language were almost unparalleled, and the trader at the margins of French imperialism that he became. The sequence that opens the 'Sleeping Dogs' section explores whether the youthful poet might have resurfaced in the Marseille hospital where Rimbaud died.

The rest of the poems in that section find voices for those who can no longer speak. The following section, 'Decaying Orbits', mostly explores the permeable borders between science and art.

As detailed in the notes that follow, the final section more directly confers 'Rights of Reply', mostly to the subjects or interlocutors of mostly well-known poems. The voices are in each case constrained to use the same end-words as were used in the original.

Notes

'Aruru contemplates her work'
Aruru was an Akkadian goddess, one of the creators of humanity from mud and their blood of a killed god. In the Epic of Gilgamesh, she created Enkidu, the future companion of Gilgamesh, from mud that she flung to the earth.

'Shamhat remembers Enkídu '
Shamhat was a sacred prostitute who was commissioned to seduce the uncatchable Enkídu from his life with the wild animals.

'Enkídu among the animals'
Enkidu, the companion of Gilgamesh, first lived among the wild animals without language and managed to evade all attempts to capture him until seduced by Shamhat.

'Gilgamesh contemplates his dual nature', 'Gilgamesh listens for the gods'
Gilgamesh was the tyrannical king of Uruk, part god and part human. The gods created Enkidu as a companion for him in an effort moderate his behaviour.

'Humbaba among the cedars'
Humbaba was the giant guardian of the Cedar Forest, one of the homes of the gods. His very appearance created terror among humans. He was attacked and killed by Gilgamesh and Enkidu.

'Shamash renounces his devotee'
Shamash was the Akkadian sun god. He was the member of the pantheon who took the greatest interest in the affairs of humanity. He helped Gilgamesh and Enkidu to defeat Humbaba, but did not intervene to save Enkidu from death.

'Uta-napishti contemplates eternal life', 'Uta-napishti's wife'
Uta-napishti is the Sumerian analogue to Noah. He and his (unnamed) wife were saved from a deluge that destroyed humanity, given eternal life and transported to the other side of the ocean.

'Rimbaud in Marseille, 1891'
Rimbaud forswore poetry in his early twenties and spent the rest of his short life as a trader and gun runner, mostly in the Horn of Africa. He died in Marseille from the complications of having a cancerous leg amputated.

'Farewell'
D J Thomas is replying to his son Dylan's Elegy for him.

'Prospero, Later'
Prospero reconsiders the epilogue to Shakespeare's Tempest.

'Good Fences Make Good Neighbours'
Robert Frost's neighbour provides his perspective on Mending Wall.

'Jean Armour's Song'
Rabbie Burns' wife contemplates what sort of love is like a red, red rose.

'Now I Am Old And White'
Maud Gonne decides not to age gracefully, maintaining her perspective on W B Yeats.

'Penelope'
Lord Tennyson provided a striving end for Ulysses. Ulysses' wife Penelope is not impressed.

'Dear Andrew'

Andrew Marvell's coy mistress shows that she was not either of those things.

'At The Summer Solstice'

Robert Graves wrote To Juan at the Summer Solstice. Juan responds.

'After The Frost'

Hartley Coleridge has views on his father's 'Frost at Midnight'.

www.ingramcontent.com/pod-product-compliance
Lightning Source LLC
Chambersburg PA
CBHW020329010526
44107CB00054B/2043